W9-CBR-037

In
the
heart
of
the
light

POETRY
OF AWAKENING

Special Extended Edition with
Self Love Practices & Rituals

Ashley Lord

In the heart of the light; Special Extended Edition
copyright © 2020 Ashley Lord

All rights reserved. No part of this book may be used or reproduced in any form without prior written permission, except in the case of brief quotations in a book review or scholarly journal.

ISBN: 978-1-7770853-3-9

Cover design by Ashley Lord & Jana Jelovac

Author Photo: Self Portrait "Sacred Forest"
Taken on a beautiful summer's day while wandering barefoot through the Limberlost Forest Reserve in Huntsville, Ontario, Canada

This Special Extended Edition was originally born in a beautiful collaboration between Ashley Lord & TheraBox, Inc.

www.ashleylord.com *@loveashleylord @intheheartofthelight @mytherabox*

We are all *alchemists*.

For my Family,
my greatest teachers,
I am deeply grateful for our love.

And for the visionaries, the dream seekers, the sensitives,
empaths and poets; I honour us.

We have the distinct privilege
of feeling our way
through this life.

May we always remember the importance
of this potent gift...

And report back,
in art.

"The moment you accept what troubles you've been given; the door will open" -Rumi

The poetic offering you hold, has come through in many moments of connection. Honouring this heart, writing it words of encouragement, connecting to its beauty, as I sat in the mud; witness to it all. Birthing this book has been deeply healing. It has been a practise of learning, unlearning, remembering and so much surrender. It has taught me how to embody resilience and allowed my tears to fall. It has brought everything to the surface as writing continues to be one of my guiding lights and purest medicines. Dancing, moving, singing sweetly to myself, channeling the words of the angels; creating all the poetry.

May it remind you of the infinite wisdom of the universe that lives within us all.

I hope it serves you.

In this *Special Extended Edition* woven among the pages of poetry you'll find invitations to pause and go a little deeper. Sprinkles of medicine offerings.

Energy Practices, Affirmations, Journaling & Ritual.
There are no right or wrong ways to navigate them, nor shall there be any specific order indicated as to what practices to do when. Consider this a *choose your own adventure of poetry and sacred self care,* blessed with the simple intention to hold space for you to meet yourself
…in the ways it feels helpful to do so.
Allow your intuitive energy and wild heart to guide you.

*Place this book upon your altar and smile,
she's already been charged for you.*
Your journey awaits.

Many blessings

We have the ability to transform. To take the pains and passions that run deep within our souls and turn them into gold. For if we are made of golden light, then may our broken hearts be but opportunities for awakening.

May we rise each day with the sun's beam like warmth filling our hearts. Holding us, so we may hold ourselves in the practices that shift our energy. Feeling into our broken spaces, so we may heal them. For when our embodied experiences stay stuck within us, we remain disconnected from truth, from light. So may we feel through the sticky and into our steadiness. Connect. See. Clearly. Expand. Our Resonance. Be here. In our soft strength. In humility and in deep compassion. Be willing to see these challenging gifts of our path as jewels that allow us to know ourselves, our essence. Awaken the wise ones, that live deep within us.

May we trust our heartache, the heartbreak of our brothers, sisters and know we are not separate. May we be present to this life, may we witness each other and know we are all connected. And we all have the ability to step onto the path, to soothe all the tender hearts with our love. Everything we ache for is here. Right here. When we are willing to walk through our fire and let it burn through the sky.

I've known struggle. My heart, broken. Into a million pieces.
I've witnessed trauma and heartbreak change me. And,
I've seen the suffering adorn me with wings that have soared into a brave armour of light. Decorated in truth. Alive to it all.

Sometimes our heartache hardens us. Fastening layers of protection around our truth. But what if these achings were our most trusted advisors? Readying us. Cracking us, open.
What if we let down our shields to set ourselves free?

What if we allowed ourselves to break out of our cages, cast ourselves to the wind and floated into the safety of love. Into this abundance, available to our hearts, at all moments;
Oh how we could fly.

Then there we are, naked. Our heart's exposed to the light.
What if only then when we are shattered, we didn't break. But chose to pick up the pieces.
To dress ourselves in light,
Like a kaleidoscope of love.
To move and turn these pieces towards eyes of warmth, to trust the wild journey in all its heartache and earthly wonder.

We are this *resilient*. We are this *beautiful*.

What a gift to move within,
A deep dive into the heart space,
To bow in prayer
To bless yourself,
And write your way towards awakening.
To tend to your energy body
To affirm, visualize and emerge
This is your magic
Right here for you to claim
As you come out and play again.

In the *heart* of the light.

THE COLLECTION

LETTERS TO MY HEART 17

THE BASEMENT SESSIONS 43

CIRCLE POEMS 57

RAINBOWS & DARKNESS 67

BLESSINGS AT DAWN 79

ASHES AND LIGHT 91

IN THE HEART OF THE LIGHT 103

FIRE AND WATER 115

THE GRANDMOTHER 123

REVOLUTION OF LOVE 141

MORNING BLOSSOM 155

POETESS, LIONESS 171

ENCORE 187

REFLECTION & PRAYER 197

We all have a light inside, an ever flowing
reservoir of love.

LETTERS TO MY HEART

Emergence

Emergence
requires stillness,
quiet
inner movement to awaken
and reclaim
the sacred light.
The towering oak alive within me
her seedling asks for shelter,
for space.
For the deepening of her roots
is nourished
and loved
in silence.

Energy Practice
Go out to your favourite place in nature and find a tree that
calls you. Sit or lay upon her roots at the base of her trunk and
breathe intentionally with her support. Deep inhales and nice
long exhales with a softened jaw and face. Allow this practice
to ground and nourish you. Remember to thank and feel
gratitude for the tree and yourself to conclude.

This Heart

Tears like golden whispers
And silent messengers
There's dew on this heart
Let words move through you now,
As heartbreak speaks
And grief awakens.

Golden Hours

For the beautiful souls
whose broken hearts
light the sky.
Trust in your light
Because, like the sun,
your golden hours
are most beautiful,
wrapped in clouds

Visualization (Energy Practice)
Imagine a most beautiful coloured sky that lives inside of you
*(pinks, reds, golds, oranges with the most majestic of clouds woven between
the colours.)* You see the clouds help to illuminate the colours
that dance across the skies of your heart. Take a moment to
welcome and thank the clouds within you *(representing all the
challenges you face both past & present)*, honour them, invite them
closer, love on them. *Now,* watch as you effortlessly see them
move away slowly and you surrender them back into the sky,
to dissolve in perfect divine timing with only love; you watch
them change shape and fade.

I feel deeply. I've been blessed with space to do the work, the work that matters. To feel into my aliveness, my heart and dive deep into the depths of my soul. To breathe. To move. To expand. I'm so proud of the beautiful places I've been. To be able to connect, to what is most alive in this heart. What requires nourishment, what needs to move, what is asking to come through me as I continue my souls work on this earth. How to thaw the layers of protection, create necessary boundaries and honour both wise elder and little child. Through deep feeling I've been blessed with insights leading me back to love. And I have learned that the most magical gift we offer each other is in the soft surrender of our own darkness. In witnessing ourselves with compassion, in tenderness. Leading from this space. *The sweetness is inside us all.* There is so much beauty here.

I'm okay
To shift the energy. To be here. To move. To remind myself it's okay to ask for help. That I am allowed to hurt. It's okay to feel pain. I will be present to the failures, the challenges, learn from these heartaches, because they are my teachers. To let them in, feel fully. I let them lead me to where I need to be. And I'm allowed to feel gratitude. The abundance of gratitude for this journey and for this wild, beautiful heart. Because it's here, in the heart of feeling, this intimacy of my experience where I get to witness this glorious life. It is all here. Right here. Where the magic is.

And it is here, where I am free.

May we unlock the wisdom of our hearts.

Energy Practice

Close your eyes, place your hands on your heart. Take a deep breath in, let it go. Do that a few times. Let a little hint of a smile come to the face. Notice the space behind the hands in the center of the chest, the energetic heart space, breath here for a few moments. Feel your wise heart. Thank yourself for this practice, taking space to breathe and for how far you've come in your journey, that you've landed here, right now, in this moment. Smile with gratitude for all the dark, the light and everything in between. For all the madness, for all the learning, for all the beauty. Smile and revel at it all. No matter what is present in your life, take this moment to be grateful for it all, soak up this moment to pause and be here with yourself, your breath and your heart. Here you are alive, breathing, making space. It is a beautiful moment to celebrate how far you've come. *Notice if your heart has any messages for you.*

A New Sun

Stacking moments
Arise,
Reminding me to stay
Another moment here
In the discomfort,
The decay.
I connect with this body
And these painful seeds
Planted moons ago,
Like bullets in my spine.
Turning trenches
Calcified
Within me,

Now I'm here to awaken
The frozen roots,
Deeply buried
From the tangled past
Their leaves wrapped and entwined,
Like thorns around this heart.
Light shines on them
Warming the thaw,
They're coming alive
To be tamed
Picked and arranged
In this new beginning
As a new sun shines,
And guides me through,
The fruitful darkness.

Affirmation
I trust that everything is unfolding perfectly in my life. All is well.

And as I gaze at the peaceful waters to my left, I see the sky, knowing the sun shines behind the winter clouds and it is still bright. There's light here as the snow falls outside and my heart is held in the blessings of this moment. Warmth.

Beauty is everywhere. Even in the hardest of moments, a little sparkle remains, to remind me, remind us, to shine. Amidst the dew of the saltiest tears and during the snottiest of seasons. We are expanding. Here, we are. Alive. *Present to it all.*

Dear sweet soul. Thank you for being here. Thank you for your journey. Thank you for trusting your heart. Thank you for curling up with these words, with yourself, in this moment. *Such magnificence is alive within you.* I know it. May this space allow the light to enter you, exactly where it needs to.

I made myself a promise. Never again will I push away my feelings. They are truth.

They are my messengers and beacons of light.

They are my inner guidance and gps of the soul. They are inspiration and honesty.

Feelings, birthing the artist who is asked to shine her light in all of its mess, glory and vibrant wonder.

It's been a journey to trust this process. To hold space for the power of my being-ness.

Nothing has ever felt more aligned then allowing the flow of *these words and my heart* to come through to you in this form.

Energy Practice & Journaling

Place your left hand on your belly and your right hand on your heart.

Take a few rounds of breath, in through the nose, out through the mouth *(if possible)*.

Relax your jaw, your shoulders, your belly and let yourself feel held here.

Ask your heart the following question and see what answers come...

What truth(s) have I been ignoring that want my attention??

Take a few moments and journal about any answers that come.

I am the wise eagle. *I am* the baby bird.

Morning Sweetness

As bells ring
Here I am
Present
To my sweetness.
Quiet mornings in
The rocking chair,
Giving my heart space
To remember.

Whole Heart, Higher Self

Loving connection with my heart
Amidst the aching
Energies pulling,
And pushing me.
The steady unsteadiness,
Move, breathe, be present
Speaks this heart
Meeting imperfection
And change,
With my whole self.

Journaling
What has been pulling me from feeling centered and possibly stirring up some inner discomfort or unrest?
First, write about it. Feel it. Secondly, write with gratitude and curiosity about its wisdom and lesson *(as a witnessing observer).*

The Six in Snow

Winter. To slow down. To move inward. To be like nature.
To take extra time to get places. This heart knows. To be
challenged with this city's pace. To curse the TTC. And wrap
up in all the scarves. The salt stained boots. And then say
screw it, and call a shared Lyft. I have a nice conversation and
a pleasant ride; watching the snow fall, peacefully. This is
Toronto. In the winter. As I honour this heart.

Sing Songbird

Songbird sing
Sweet melodies,
escape your soul
As a gift of electric
Love.
Fly high
Songbird as your
Essence dives and swoons
In movement and sound.
Songbird, symphonies
Tickle wounded hearts
And tired eyes.
Uplift us songbird
With a dance born
Only from that heart
In this form.
Spin and twinkle
As you shine brighter,
Softly in surrender.

On Retreat

The morning light,
Meeting the day
In quiet
On retreat.
As the snow
Softly falls
We emerge
From our slumber
To greet this day.
We sit in peace,
Move in love,
And surrender to
The wisdom
That meets us
Exactly as we are.
We make space
For rest,
For ease.
Nourishing our souls
In the cozy quiet
Of mother natures
Wintery embrace.

You are made of golden light. Remember this.
Trust this.

Full Moon Practice

Sit with yourself or in a gathering of souls,
Speak aloud what is present for your heart.
Take your time,
Listen, fully.
Hold yourself in this space,
Hold each other.
Pause,
Sit quietly,
Feel the heart.
Write down what is moving through
What is being asked to let go...

Continue,
To be here.
Breathe.
Take the paper,
Burn to dust.
While humming a sweet tune
Of gratitude.
Sprinkle the ashes
Into the water
Under the moonlight
Feel this blessing
Of new beginnings
And trust,
In this surrender.

Ritual

Under the light of the full moon, bring yourself into sacred ceremony by lighting a candle and sitting with the intention of making space to let go what is not serving you. Read this *Affirmation Prayer* (below) aloud to yourself:

I sit with myself
And hold myself here in love, under the light of the moon
I pause, I sit quietly,
All is well.
I remember that all is unfolding perfectly for me
And I remember it's okay to let go of all that is not serving
my highest good, the highest good.
Under the light of the moon, I trust that it's safe to surrender any fears
that may be holding me back, any habits that are no longer helpful and
any experiences that I'm ready to let go of, knowingly and unknowingly.
I am here, under the moon and I am safe to feel.
I feel my heart, and all that's moving through it and I am safe.
I trust that I begin anew under the light of this moon.

Sit in silence for a few minutes. Write down your feelings onto a piece of paper in the following reflection and intention:

"What needs to move through me? What am I ready to let go of?"

(this could be ways of being with yourself, ways you show up in the world, ways you do things, patterns, habits, negative self-talk, relationships etc.)

Take the paper into a bowl, burn it fully. Go outside under the moon and sprinkle the ashes upon the earth as an offering and reminder to your heart that it's safe to surrender and begin again. *Move forward a little lighter and into the next cycle :)*

For the tender hearts.
It's okay to be scared, nervous.
Anxious. Angry. Panicked.
Sit with it.
Be here.
With what is present.
Right now.
Stay in the space.
Maybe breathe into your belly,
Or put on some music
And tend to yourself,
Sit with it,
Right here
To shift the energy,
By meeting yourself
Exactly as you are.
You don't have to run,
You're safe here in the madness.
As you visualize warmth surrounding you
Softening you.
Choosing love in presence
In the heartache,
And all that it's teaching you.

Believe in your light.
Trust your light.
Nourish your light.

I love you like the sky painted in stars.

May you always trust your heart. May you be with yourself and trust that *life is happening for you.* And when you answer the call to honour the feelings born of truth, that this is the beauty, where the magic comes to live through you.

In this glorious life. It's heartaches. The hardships. All those disguised boxes of love wrapped in funky ribbons. The ones reminding us to let go of judgement and be kind. So that we may remember. To lean in. To do the work. The work, that connects us. To presence. Oneness, peace. And to light.

Because this magic,
All it's magnificence...

It lets the heart beam like the light of a hundred million diamonds dancing in the sun.

And so it is.

A few years ago, I lived in a tiny home, in the quaintest of neighbourhoods, a house across from the park, in a basement, below a writer, where I wrote. And wrote some more. Every night. This magical place, I entered through a garden, where my front foyer was a laundry room and my heart breathed poetry into the wee hours. A little haven of carpeted earth. To hold a heart that was broken. I wrote myself lullabies and *put the pieces back together*, one poem at a time.

THE BASEMENT SESSIONS

Blank space

electric through these
Walls,
Burn brighter bold
Sky,
Poke at the
Universe.
Here the words
Shapeshift,
Movement exchanged in space
The stealth unknown
Breathes
White space among
Us.

Lunar Growth

Dreams exposed
In light
Extract wishes,
Unearthed shadows
Cast of necessity
As diamonds await
The sun.
Pink sky in bloom
This kaleidoscope path
Widens,
As patient gems
Pause in darkness
Under pressure,
To refract & rise.

In this place

Sleeping &
stretching
The nights into days,
Beneath the city's
Ground.
Immersed in a writer's
World.
Electric through these
Walls,
There are two of us
Letting inner worlds escape
In dust lit rooms
Treading,
Without a single
Step.

The Moss

Stay here with me
For a chance to listen,
As we write the
Future
Staying up
all night.

A familiar place,
Let me exist here
Where the music is,
And in the hearts
Of the other
Rolling stones.

A moment to fly

Birds,
Where bright lights
Are not.
Sound,
Where silence
Aches.
Follow this path
removed of earth.
Can we remain here
In moments
Too soon undone?
Much less ordinary
Be it unveiled
But only,
Where the light is.

Roots

Placed on a floor
Of carpeted earth.
These basement nights
Shape me.
Pressed,
As textured memories
Resemble aged tapestries,
Broken strands
Once woven.
Pierced,
As golden waves
Offer sound.
Bold notes,
Fade out
Home,
unbroken here.
This heart grows
Roots,
Where the music is.

Affirmations
I am safe | I am grounded | I am not my past | I am here
I am alive in this moment | I am the sweetest melody
I am made of music | I am rooted
I am at home in myself.

Twilight Becomes

The days draped in light
Fulfill dream states
Unstated.
Sleep, not for the
longing of
Heart calls,
In angelic sounds
Pronounced beyond
The blazing strong
Twilight.
To be unknown
In becoming,
Dare not to run.

Cracks in the Mirror

Bask in complexion
This flickering boldness
Dims perception,
And develops
faces.

To raise truth at
Smoked mirrors,
Catching
Glimpses of
the unseen

Ray of Love

Guardian of light
Your beauty glows
Goddess energy,
Emits rays of love
As you dance
In the journey.
The hands of healing
You hold
To nourish the world,
Surrender soft silent
Nights
Shining star.
Your wishes are dreams
Uncomplicated,
Blessed in knowing
You are here
To serve.
Like the smile
of a
Sweet child.

Wandering Truth

Fascinate the subtle
Hum of stillness,
Drawn near to
The place
Where shadows
Exhibit
Relics of
Broken hearts.
Breaking tales
Amongst dogs
Woes.
Sharing stories
Un-aimlessly
For the wanderer
Follows merrily,
Confusing truths.

Cinematic Element

Stillness speaking in
Recycled whispers,
Imagine words in
Bleak vision.
Find me here
In the heat of a
Winterless dream.
Unarmed pleas in
Soft seeking
Thinking pushed with
Warm air,
Electric fires linger
In the shoveling of
Fables untold.

Bellows Blow

The story was as so.
at twenty something a
delicate inquiry of intrigue
unknown.
astounded at the bend in the river
she dove,
in deep visions
pulling towards light's reflection
the sun's gleam stilled ripples,
oh carry her until she woke.

it was all unknown, until it was so.
dreamers dream at thoughts
below, a riptide bellows blow.
frosted waters the mistress skated,
across dark veils of silk rainbows
emerging into gold.
and it was so.
and it was so.
and she broke to know things unknown.

And from the depths the love will glow,
uncovering wishes, like windows to the soul.
weighed in feathers dipped in memories
of which life's mystery kindly bestowed…

why do bellows blow?
for flames ignite sparks as
come the rains, un-taming this love
lays awake and must forgo.

Gratitude

Trust the process
Dear sweet souls,
How blessed we are to be
Present to it all.

CIRCLE POEMS

Love Blooms

Love blooms quietly
Like the flowers
Of spring
Naturally colouring
The landscape.
My heart
Smells the patient
Fragrance of
Something too
Beautiful
To be rushed.
This colourful love,
May it bloom for seasons
To come.

Journaling
What is blooming in your life right now?

New Life

Bursting bright lights
Fade bruises.
Hearts passions push
Spaces between,
Persistent ridges & tears
Become smooth.
There is new life here.

New Light Sewn

In the light of the morning
It was bright.
The day broke
Again & new sun
Refreshed tired eyes.
The light melted hard edges
& smoothed rough memories.
Tattered thoughts
Turned into tapestries,
This beginning adorned
With tassels
Sewn from that
Once broken heart.
The pieces a little shinier,
Put back together
Differently

Dancing Dreams

When the rain comes
Let it flow,
Do not dwell
upon the drops,
For no storm
Unheard the thunder roar.
Their round essence
Glow like the face
To the sun.
Warmed & dressed up,
Like the thought of you
And your dancing dreams.
The inspiration of mind waves
Gleam & poke.
Speak truth again
As the fade of the night,
Turns the hum of the day
Into visions
Of times difference.
When our heads rest
At mindful hours parted,
And straight to the heart.

Is there a storm, a situation, in your life currently passing through that could have a message for you? What is it?

Ritual:
Put on some music that calls you in this moment; dance and move your body to meet the energy of this situation in your life, dance, dance and dance some more. Let yourself really feel the energy of it. Let yourself feel any waves of emotion come up and move through you. Do this for about 10 minutes. Then lay down and rest for 10 minutes.
Journal about your experience.

Time

Drop off
The suspension
Swiftly
Causing drifting
Appetites.
Two wild hearts
Ages old and
Aching.
Guitar melodies
Smooth
The quiet mind.
Rest not sleep,
Circling casted grooves
In spite of time
Uninvested.

Shall we get
Lost in
The
Winter?
While the
Sun's fade
Is ever glowing.

Let's wear *sweatpants*
At board meetings
Because
I wouldn't change
A thing.

To be unknown
in becoming,
Dare not to run.

Affirmations
I am exactly where I need to be in this moment
All is unfolding perfectly for my highest good

Rubble on my heart,
The film where stickiness
Pulls me down
Wanting to escape,
To break free
Of the chains
Unto myself.
I have the key
To these shackles
Of unexpressed fear,
Only I may surrender
The emotions
Keeping this heart
Locked up tight.
I am not defined by this rage,
I am not my grief
But it's mine to express
To shout from the rooftops
I'm here, it matters!
This broken heart
Needs a hand to hold,
A vase to smash
As the sunlight still shines
Onto the dust
That has settled
On my soul,
For long enough.

RAINBOWS AND DARKNESS

Doubt

I listen to my heart,
what it's asking
And when doubt creeps in
I slow down, I connect again.
Get right into that space
The heart of the desire
Meet it again,
and welcome it as truth.
And then I thank doubt
For showing me the way,
To where I needed to go.

Rainbows & Darkness

In this place
Where the mask's
Shadows widen.
On the other side
Of love
Energy flows,
Dangerously into
Uncharted waters,
The dark side
of bliss.
Where we celebrate
Wounded wings
Cast behind the
Rainbows.

Remember it's okay to not have all the answers.

Radical, Self love.

Journaling
What does radical Self love look and feel like for you?

The road we leave behind us must be honoured, as much as the one before us. As we let go of the pieces of ourselves that no longer serve our highest good, here we are sometimes with more questions than answers. What must we let go of? What needs space? How can we celebrate more? Move with grace, love all our parts, our journey? So I reflect, and as I move forward into the new, I find myself hearing the words of my teachers, "to love all the pieces of me, every single one". Even the parts I'm ready to give up, promote to new ways of being; more aligned ways of loving myself. All of the hurts, pains, challenges, triumphs and the questions.

To love everything. Because the point is to love it all. And as beautifully written by one of my favourite poets:

"To be patient to all that is unresolved in your heart and try to love the questions themselves, like locked rooms and like books that are written in a very foreign tongue. Do not now seek the answers, which cannot be given you because you would not be able to live them. And the point is, to live everything. Live the questions now. Perhaps you will then gradually, without noticing it, live along some distant day into the answer"
                                                                    -Rainer Maria Rilke

And so my wish for myself, for us, is to be gentle with our hearts. To be kind and patient with ourselves as we continue to move forward, with all the big questions and dreams alive in us. To love ourselves fully, through it all. May we love all that's come before us and all that we leave behind. All that we've loved, learned, lost and let go of. Let us revel in the mystery of magic that's yet to unfold as we are here, in the beauty of now, standing, resting, in this moment. To pause. Here. To trust, as we step forward into presence, again and again, this continuing, in the midst of all it's shadows and heartache, that we are here. We are awakening. We are one. Celebrate and rejoice. For we are living life. Moment by moment. And all we have is this.

Journaling
What are you favourite ways to celebrate?

Moments

Sounds of quiet
Flickering candles
Pause,
And glazed eyes are still.
For it is always in stillness
Where soft smiles
Emit
Light beams
Of truth.
As dark becomes light
There are no constants,
And moments are cherished.

Everyone has a story of struggle
from their past...
But we all have the opportunity
to write the magical tale
of our future.

Journaling

Take some space to reflect on the last few chapters of your life...if you were writing your memoir, what would the names of each of the chapters be? Then imagine the names of the chapters of your life that are not yet written....What would you title them?? (Have fun with this!)

It's amazing how powerful it is to let my guard down and let another being hold my heart. When I'm at my most vulnerable I retreat inwards. This has been a practice I've perfected over the years. It's been so necessary at times. I'm rewriting this story. For as I awaken, as my heart heals and opens, I find the most beautiful moments of healing in shared connection with others. We're social creatures. And as a wise teacher once said to me, "we are hurt in relationships, so we must heal in community." And it's okay to be here, open, raw, exposing my heart, trusting this moment. *Messy. Human.*

Energy Practice:
Is there a tough conversation you've been avoiding, but feeling you want to have with someone? Before you have the conversation, take a few minutes to ground and center yourself (maybe this means a meditation, a walk outside in nature, breathwork, some essential oils, you choose)
Then, have the (rather uncomfortable sweaty talk)
Notice how you feel afterwards and if your energy has shifted at all.
Celebrate yourself for speaking your truth.

Oh dear heart
Your wounds close to the surface
Today so fresh and fragile.
I know the overwhelm that runs so
Steadily along your bones,
But please believe me that you
Can have space from this worry,
You can know light along the way,
True healing is your birthright.
Lean into the discomfort,
Trust the love that others share with you
Let them hold you.
Let yourself be held,
For it is in these moments
Where you can feel into oneness
And know that *love is the only road*
And all you'll ever need.

Energy Practice
Tapping or Emotional Freedom Technique (EFT)
To shift anxiety & overwhelm, to encourage safety and
relaxation in the body (*please find details on page 204*)

Here I am. In this place, writing these words, compiling this book. The universe encouraging me with her whispers, again and again, to offer this poetic alchemy. To follow my highest truth. To do what sparks my soul. Where I've set all the rules on fire and *loving myself fully* has become the new business plan.

Journaling
Where in your life might you feel like you need to set all the rules on fire?

BLESSINGS AT DAWN

Choices made
We must sit with the rippled effects,
We must do so honestly
We must always choose love.

Blades of Truth

A mind with blind soldiers
Goes to battle with herself.
Build not walls of protection.
Learn the art of your sword and
Speak only blades of truth.

Meditation helps us build awareness.
From that awareness we learn how to take care of ourselves.
And how to show up in the world.

Energy Practice
Perhaps more softness is necessary.

A simple meditation, sit or lay down, arranging the body in a way that feels comfortable and supported. Take three deep cleansing breaths (in nose, out mouth) and then let the breath slowly return to a more organic rhythm. Bring your attention to the two little rings of skin around each nostril. Notice the air of the natural breath moving in and out of the nose. Notice the temperature, notice the pace, just notice. No judgement. Just notice. Do this for 1-3 minutes to start.

Find more guided practices to help you shift your energy, soften and build awareness. **AshleyLord.com/meditations**

There is much learning here
Many lessons
That lead us back to love.
This challenging beautiful path
Of the awakened life.
But my darling,
Find joy in the shadow
And follow it into the light.
Because…
You are light.

Affirmations
I trust my shadow
I am made of light

Beauty born
From
Chaotic ashes,
Rise up to
the light.
Golden wing tipped
Dreams
Dipped in
Blessings
At
Dawn.

This Life

This life
In all her beauty
Blessings
And lessons.
Forever humbled
Grateful
This divine mystery
As I greet each new day
With the curiosity
And wide eyes.
For life is happening
For me,
For us
To shed the layers
That shield our hearts,
And return us to
Love.

Love let me

Love let me share this voice
In the heart,
Elevating
This inner healer
Awakens,
Her Butterfly soul
Cleansing wounds
Of untapped mystery
Emerging
In offering.

My heart belongs
To the golden
Mornings
In soft surrender
As the universe reminds me
Of peace
And how to share
My light.

Morning Practice

Soft music hums
The fire's movement
And the remnants of
Tea cups and candles
Beside my mat.
This practise
So steady,
An extension of me.

Morning,
Working out the kinks
Aligning energetically
This is the beauty
Unveiling
Spacious practise
Setting boundaries
So that when I wake,
I also RISE.

Journaling
Do you have a favourite morning practice?
Are you doing it every morning? Do you want to be?

Yes: celebrate, celebrate, keep going
No: celebrate, celebrate this awareness, then ask yourself *what might need to change to make space for it?*

Follow Ash on Instagram *@loveashleylord* or connect with me in my Sacred Self Care Community for more **guidance & support with your morning rituals** xo

Harmony's Clock

It's as if there
is no time
only sweet space
When I write.
Like I could stay here
In this beingness.

For when the
Sun appears
From beyond the horizon
Her morning glow
Greets me
With a smile.

This heart,
She laughs
Like it was etched upon
Her face as a buddha
Bathing in the water
With flowers upon her soul.

As if to say
Slow down
I'm here, Dear one
May poems move
Through you now
In freedom and timeless wonder.

Turning the clock
Of this earthly realm
With a nod,
A sparkled wink in my eye
In the faith of continuing

ASHES AND LIGHT

Oh wise words, the keeper of a humble heart.

Meditation; the *key* to the heart of the universe.

Bask,
In the heavenly
Beauty
Of
Magic
In all that is
Here,
Breathe sweet soul,
All we have is this

Energy Practice
Pause here, in this moment.
Look around, see, feel and hear what is around you.
Soak it in.
Thank yourself for paying attention.

My wings
Were ready
When I didn't think I was.
Heartache broke me
Again, and again.
I was being asked
To lean into love
To let the ashes of
Learning
Burn, to awaken
Me.
So that I could
Rise
And continue
Learning.
With a little more love
And a lot less suffering,
To be with compassion
And let kindness speak
Through me.
And now,
I hang my heart
Right here,
Where
The light is..

Affirmations
My wings are ready | I am made of light
I love myself | I accept myself | I honour my journey

My light shines the brightest
When I'm true to this heart.

Journaling
What does it feel like in my body to be true to my heart?

A gaze into the mirror
Looking at you
Through my eyes of love
Darling
After a good cry
And watching those birds
At the lake
Glide along the calmly rippled water
Speaking simple truths
Of delights that soothe
And inform,
How to love you better

Oh human.
Seeking
Complicates
And weathers
The blue skies.
For if we all
Unarmoured our hearts
With a little more
Sunshine in the light
A wag of our tails
At the dark,
Perhaps
We'd come to
Be
A little less
Worried.
Keeping in mind
These subtle
whispers from angels
Reminding us,
That
It just
Doesn't
Matter.

Blooming & Becoming

The dreamer is awake
Yet discomfort comes
And doubt stirs
This bright heart.
Consumed by shadows cast
As it sparks the accent,
On this return to love.

To trust the wise
Vibrant knowing
That exists beyond the
Shadows of fear.
I begin, in this moment
In the unwavering truth of presence
Where everything ends

And begins again.
Here, there is no grasping
But a silent smile of gratitude
For the unknown,
And the aliveness
That rests
In not knowing.

Be with blooms
Of peace,
They're awake and
Unwavering
With every breath
Of salty love
And sweet surrender.

Sitting here.
In the space between breaths.
Channeling words of luminance.
Of warmth.

Moving the energy.

Ascending to Love

What beauty, in the unfolding of our hearts, our gifts.
Letting out *all* of ourselves, from the safe shelter and into
All that we've imagined, wished & dreamed.
Into the *light* of our best life.
This is the real work.
What is alive in your heart?
What must you surrender to come fully into bloom?
Where is the fear?
Are you staying curious to it all?
Being kind to yourself?
May you share your wildness and feel the full power of your beingness.
May you trust your journey; all that shows up for you.
The sacred divine timing of all that was. All that is, and will come to be.
You are pure potential. You are pure light.
You are here to *make waves and touch hearts*.

Journaling
With love in your heart, softly answer the questions above in your favourite journal.

I've been writing, oh yes. Everyday in fact. In my sweet abode. Channelled words of divine. Of warmth. Moving the energy. As I let go of attachment, trust my instincts and with them a deep knowing of the creation coming to be. This book. Yes. This pocketbook of remembering. These words, but an offering. Letting go of what it all means and trusting who it's meant for. Connecting hearts. As I follow my own.

IN THE HEART OF THE LIGHT

"The first caterpillar to turn into a butterfly must have been like...
Yoooooooooooo!"
-unknown.

A Blessing of Light

A friendship of love
this journey continues
In the continuing
In the shifting
In the changing,
As you bring
more laughter
To a forested land.
Your heart is
Called home
Again
And again.
And we are but blessed
In this magic,
This mystery
Of the unfolding
Of light, love
And wonder.
And all that
Remains
Is but a dream
To be seen.
May you be blessed
On this path ahead.
Wise spirit,
Soul sister
Female divine,
I bow to you.

It's April Now

When my light gets dim
Sometimes
I eat bagels with cream cheese
Gluten free of course
And indulge in overpriced decaffeinated
Sugary beverages
To ease my heart.
This is my truth today
Many days lately.
As I sit bundled up
In a sweater and 2 blankets,
Don't forget the scarf
That hasn't left my neck

It's April now
And it's bloody cold still
It's pretty grey
And I'm loving myself more.
Smiling in the simple delights
Of bagels and hot beverages,
Allowing instead of judging
These yearnings for pleasure
Because I ain't getting it from
This city life,
Concrete jungle games
And wondering...
Maybe I'll write a little longer
And let my light charge.

Woman aka Wildflower

Wildflower,
Show me your heart
Dance me your love
And surrender
Your woes upon my soul.
For I am here to hold you
Wildflower.
Your shaky truths
Fascinate me.
A collection of your
Fears
But an illusion
Wildflower,
It's okay,
To love where you may not be welcome
To bend towards the light
We are here to let each other
Grow
And bury our roots deep
So when we're pulled
We're not torn.
And wildflower,
May you grow freely
Through the cracks
That have allowed you
To forge your own
Path
And bloom
into the warmth.

May you smile with the truth of the sun's light reflected in a thousand beautiful rainbows.

Lean In

Living from the heart
What a wonderful space
Where there is freedom
Connection
To divine
Wisdom.
The universe
Holds
The
Most powerful
Of space

For us to lean in
And come alive,
Because
Alignment
With our souls
Destiny,
Our purpose,
Our many purposes
The spark in our heart
where everything is
Made of gold.

And where there is light,
there is dark.
So, I'm not afraid
When shadows
Cast upon
This heart

Block me
From
Truth
I believe
That the darkest
Moments
Are those
With the highest
Potential
To shape shift
And change
As
The alchemists
We are.
Liberating our light
Again, and again.

Not always
Do I feel
Like a unicorn
Of love,
But I know it is
My essence
Rooted deep
This divinity
That breathes
Within me
Is here,
In every moment.

When I'm not feeling
Like the most
Vibrant version
Of myself
For whatever reason
Tired

Sugar hangover
Self doubt
Or shame
Unsteady, in
Any of the things
That pull me from
Center.
Here
these beautiful
Opportunities
Await,

To align with truth again
Shift my energy
in that deep
Place
Of knowing
Myself.
Knowing truth,
And this energetic body
Better than anyone,
I know what I need
I trust my heart

A cup of tea
A bath
Quiet time alone
To dance
Sing
Make sound
Make art
Make love
Water plants
Share a conversation
Lay still
Move freely

Practise yoga
Meditation
Go swimming,
Or for a walk
Be in nature
Write my dreams.

I have created a life
That is blessed
In dedication
To knowing, better yet, tending,
To my energy
First.
So that
I may show up
With the best of me,
And remember
That when I'm running at
60 percent
Even 50
That I am enough.
It IS enough
Because all that
Matters
Is presence,
Exactly as I am.
The intention
Of listening,
sharing,
being
Fully available
To myself,
To others.
A human being
Living in this
Physical body

Doing the things,
Sharing the love
Waking up
Again and
Again
To the peace
The abundance
Of
Joy
That exists
Here
For us
All
To believe in each
Other
And share the
Love,
To trust
And share
Our own
Unique sparkle
Of light
That we
Are meant to
Shine
On the
World...

Journaling
How have I/can I lean in to the unsteady parts of me and
cultivate more love?

Breath
By breath.
Moment by moment.
I am here.
And
Here
We
Are.

FIRE & WATER

"when you grasp a hot stone in anger, you're the one who gets burned."
-Buddha

Who are you grateful for?
Who reflects back to you the pain that asks for tending, for
healing?
Who gets under your skin?
Can you see love in their eyes, the opportunity they offer you,
to shed fear?
To elevate.
To choose love and *raise your own vibration.*

Journaling
With love in your heart, softly answer the questions above in
your favourite journal.

Let the anger flow through.
Everything is teaching you.
Be kind, stay humble and forgive.

Poetry Lustre

A little girl lived in me, once ripened in anger
Holding charged up memories
depositing elevated value,
costing her love.
A stubborn flow into farewells did turn;
easier to mask the feels,
than willingly navigate electric unsteady.

Building shields,
thickened like an army of hearts
who could not invade her closeted walls.
A heavy shadowed weight upon her back,
Her cloaked hollows
Blackened in ash
From the fires of old.
Too much equity in protection
Gains little lustre.

The lion's mane burning
Checkered punches
Like peonies
written on
Forgotten pastured plains.
Please poetry,
smoke us out of this box
And into the wild.

Sweet Jewel of Light

There are no words
That describe the pulse
In my chest
When I see you smile.
The light in your eyes,
The wave of goodness
that washes over
Everyone you touch.

Sometimes I wish they knew
What you went through
To arrive where you are.
How proud they'd be
Of all you'd overcome,
The aches of fire
On your insides
Like an extension of me.

Felt in the depths
Of my being
I've cried for you,
Our tears like jewels of light
That helped me
Find my way back to you,
To us, to honour
Our unbreakable bond

And all our
Invisible scars
Known not
to seeking eyes
But kept safe
Within our hearts
To remind us,
Of our resilience.

Energy Practice
With who in your life do you share an unbreakable bond? The
kind of love that comes from the depths of your soul. Write
about this person in gratitude for the love you share. Read your
words again and again to invite in the love you share. Imagine
them sitting across from you right now and sending them love.
Bathe in this frequency of sweetness.

May you always know love,
and feel the steadiness of your own inner waters,
as you gaze softly at the reflection
of your divine essence, your beauty.
To know you are enough, exactly as you are.
And you can stay here. In the space between the light and the
dark.
In compassion. In love.
For our hearts were born to light the path.
Show us the way.
To lean in. We are this brave. And we are allowed to meet
ourselves.
Right here

THE GRANDMOTHER

Peaks & Valley's

In the clearing
Of the darkest spaces
Resting within,
The ones that grip
And tug
At the spirit,
In their liberation
And surrender
We wash & purify
To leave a residue of peace.
A strength
And steadiness
Unexplainable
In the mind,
Only felt in the
Depths
Of this wise heart.
In the most humble
Of gratitude
Bowing to the
Beauty,
As the layers
Balance and arrive
To awaken
Our brothers
And sisters
Holding hands
In prayer
For humanity…

And our mother,
For all her gifts
And wisdom
Of earth, sky & light.
May we stand strong
In this
Sacred space
For the welfare
Of this planet,
all her
Inhabitants.
And for the peaks and valleys
That teach us,
With love.

Ritual Salt Release *(You'll need to gather a small bowl of salt, I like using Sea salt or Himalayan salt is nice)* Feel free to fancy up this salt bowl in any way that feels helpful, you can place flowers, herbs or essential oils in the bowl with the salt. Whatever feels good to you. Create sacred space *(whatever that means for you, I like to do this by lighting a candle.)* Place the bowl of salt beside you in your sacred space. Ask your higher self to release any darkness you may be holding right now (that is not serving you) to move through you and down into your hands. Sit or rest for a moment and visualize this denser energy releasing and flowing right into the hands. Now, take the salt from the bowl and begin to rub it around your hands, absorbing all of this energy into the salt. Continue this process until it feels complete. Lastly, take the salt to the nearest water source *(nature is best, but a bath, sink or toilet are also great!)* and release the salt + energy it holds, into the water offering a few words of gratitude *(speaking them out loud or in your heart)* as a blessing to this energy that will now be recycled by the earth. "I release this to the universe, with love."

The Gratitude of Her Eyes

Elders dear
And the
Keepers
Of this medicine.
Gratitude moves
Through
Me as I
Stare into my
Mothers
Eyes.
Feeling her, with
A rebirthed calm.
Unspoken,
This sense
Of acknowledgement.
Her instincts
Trust my steadiness
Now.
And this
Existence

Of our truths
Mirrored back
To each other.
I witness
Her ease
In my own.
The music
Flowing through us,
This connection,
Unbreakable
Through space
And time…

The gratitude
Of her eyes
And this beautiful
Family of chosen
Souls.
We are safe
Here
To love amidst
All our
Darkest spaces.
All that flows between
In the depths of
Our inner
Waters,
As they
Reflect
The sparkle
Of
This
Life.
And the
Treasures,
That await
Us all.

The Moon & The Hummingbird

Beach side
Activations
These iridescent
Souls
Float,
In communion
With the
Sky.
Under stars
Holding us
Calling us
To align
As we
Speak,
To the dandelion
Wishes
Blown
Into
Our laps…

This eloquence
And *grace,*
As they beam
And sing
Humming
As the birds
Are called
To meet
Us here.
And we rise,
Retracing
The sand worn
Paths of our
Elders.
On this land
Their home,
For many moons.

Drinking the Daffodil

Our sight
Is clear
When the
Bowls sing
And sound,
Their resonance.
Pulling and
Calling my heart
Closer
This soul,
Her wisdom
Attuned
Beside sweet
Vibration,
And in emptiness
I scoop up
Calm, between
Threatened stillness
Alive within
The seas of
These waters…

Offered up
Again into
The daffodils cup,
I drink this
Peaceful
Nectar
Tasting the
Sweetness
That breathes
Within
Me,
Remembering
again,
Her offerings.

The Magnetic City

Thank you
Beauty
of the lands
And the
Bustles
of city life.
As I continue
To move
& flow
Like the
Lion
Following the
River, in
Her eyes
As the garland
Of flowers
Upon her mane
Plant seeds
Of sweetness,
To remain
When
Touched
by the
Roaring energies
Of wildness.
I make
My arrival
Across the…

Queens metal lines,
Magnetic, my own
Energies drawn
To surrender
Steady frequencies
Upon the
Battened down
Lashes
Of those
With sad eyes.
Their hearts
Locked
From the dew
Dripping
Down their
Cheeks,
Those eyes
Showing us
The way
Back to
The light.
Offering
Kisses,
To soothe these
Tired minds,
And weathered
gardens.

The Big Love

electric,
this body
moves
in waves.
these blessed
feet, inviting
the earth in
to sound;
manifesting
ecstatic movement.
to free dreams
and raise truth,
pulsing
in rhythms
opening,
the goddess dragon
breathes
fire into
light,
for the tribes
to sing
in community
as dancing
hearts
rise
together.

I am committed to building a world where we get to pay attention. Where there is space. Where there is freedom. Equality. Where we can be safe to name how we feel and if we're not okay, we ask for help. And get it. No judgement. I want to live in a world where others can hold us in all our powerful expressions, darkness and light. Where we are not too much and our fierce intensity is welcomed. Where our differences are not all that different and the truth of our light shines above it all. I want to live in a world where we are not afraid to show up for ourselves, for each other, especially when it's uncomfortable. Where we are committed to doing the work of opening our hearts, healing. So that we may put our egos aside, be with compassion and always choose love. I want to live in *this brave world*.

I am committed to tending to my own heart and energy so I may arrive in greater harmony in all my relationships. I am not doing it perfectly and neither will you, but in this inevitable imperfection may we continue to be o p e n, *aware* of our triggers, present to our blind spots and hold space for ourselves, so we may hold space for each other.

And as spoken by my beautiful teacher Seane,

"Ignore the story and see the soul. And remember to love. You will never regret it." -Billy *(Revolution of the Soul, Seane Corn)*

We all have this capacity,
to choose love.
The revolution starts with us.
Inside our hearts.
In showing up.
In paying attention.
In looking at what is.
In choosing to shift the energy.
In practise.
In healing.
In forgiveness.
In love.

And in the spaces where
there are both dark and bright,
May we rise from the ashes & bend towards the light.

We're all on
A beautiful
Journey.
May we speak only compassion
And warmth to our own
Inner waters.
May we connect
Deeply with Self
To honour
Our darkness,
Ease our hearts,
To know
Kindness.
May we be committed
In coming together,
Supporting each other
In doing the work.
To heal all the places
Where we are disconnected
from love.
May we
Feel into our
Light
And shine
It outwards
To the world,
For the welfare
Of
All beings.

It is a constant remembering. Reminding myself to chase what sets my soul on fire. To choose love. To forget about the allure of creating something shiny in the hopes it will bring me abundance. Or building out a series of carefully constructed offerings that makes perfect logical sense. I remind myself to just be me. To learn from the shadows. To share my truth in ways it feels so aligned I couldn't not do it. To share my words, these thoughts, channelled in love. To trust they are leading me to where I need to be. To be the poet. To be free to dance and spin and shine into the hearts that need these prayers. To speak for the light. To be the light. Without trying to do it perfectly, or get it right. To just put it out there, unafraid of repeating the word light a million times over. This is my truth. This is my faith. This is trust. This is pure freedom. I surrender dear universe. The words come in offering. Again, and again. Thank you. Thank you. Thank you. Bowing.

So I ask you, dear one....

What sets your soul on fire?

Journaling

With love in your heart, softly answer the questions above in your favourite journal.

REVOLUTION OF LOVE

Shake & Soar

Those times when
I share my voice, my truth,
These offerings that flow
& arrive, as if by
Surprise to my body.
It shakes.
Nervous system adjusts
As if to acknowledge the importance
Of showing up, answering the call,
Of saying yes.

Opening to the possibility
That the fierce river that runs
Within me is ready,
To flood
Into the spaces asking for water,
To awaken and nourish
Tiny seeds planted
Within the heart,
The ones you feel…
You know the ones.
Their essence awakening in us all
Our gifts to share,
Love to offer,
Extending out of us,
Moving,
like the tail of the shooting star…

May we have the courage
To walk through our fire
And let it
Burn through the sky.
To land in our truth
For when we shake, we soar
As we are becoming,
Flowing,
Towards
The sky that pokes out from the universe.

And when Sailing through choppy
Waters
With angel wings upon our backs,
Here our fears lift right up from our chest,
So we can drop them into the water
As an offering
Of peace
to our unstoppable spark,
The one that scares us down to our core
That same one that fuels the tiniest flame
into a roaring wildfire of feeling
Leaving us unimaginably alive,
Ready to claim our destiny.

On the Mat

This is for the remembering.
This is for the connection
Found in the opening of
This heart's locket
Revealing
Pictures of truth.
Helping me see,
Letting me hold and love this soul
Through the stories. Through it all,
Everything is teaching me. And I surrender again and again
To the remembering of who I am,
Burning off the tensions that grip
And the aches that dwell in my spirit and dull my soul
Each piece a loving fragment of knowing.
Moving to un-know and teach this heart again how to be free
and soar strongly.
With eyes up and heart open.
In this space - stepping into this moment,
Returning again to the mat, the cushion, to Self.
These practices
Like steady containers holding me here,
So that I may lean into discomfort.
Releasing my wings and reclaiming my light…

A Writing From 7/10/19

And every time I step again, on to that mat
When I'm stuck and seek the steadiness
That holds me
And I lean in, to the aches and the stickiness,
The residue of my dharma.
The tears
Greet this body
As if to open a dam, a gateway,
To the most beautiful
Waterfall,
Shimmering lake
And magnetic sky.
It's in the bowing
In the reverence
For all that's
Past, all that's to come,
But all that's here
In this moment
Teaching my heart
To rise
Again,
To meet the qualities of love
Forgiveness and surrender
Forever
Holding me in this essence
And I bend again
Towards that light…

With a nod to the lessons
The awakening that
Comes for me
Like a bat outta hell.
This journey, these offerings of divinity
I bow again,
I do not judge their intensity
But rather connect
To the collection of wild
Blessings that I
Have the privilege to work with,
Harmonize,
Transmute
For the global shift,
The consciousness movement
Of the revolution,
The rise
Of being,
The revolution of love.

Wolf Heart

Her embodiment
And blessings
Are among us
On this earth.
Barefoot
We walk
Across the sands & stones,
Tending to our
Hearts,
With angelic
Sounds and tones.
These soothing
Sweet
Melodies of love,
May we know the
Sweetness from
Above,
Feel into the spaces asking
Us to lean in,
Uplift the
Veils, these
Messages herein.
Teachings that
Awaken us,
Humbling our
Hearts a must,
As we move
And flow
With the tides…

The depth, our
Inner waters and cries.
May we remember
To sing them lullabies,
To swoon
And grace, through this
Dark | place.
And choose
The white wolf
In this space |
At the centre
Of our chest
Here, our magic,
It does rest.
This wolf
Within,
Her heart
It sings
As we begin
To
See again.

Shadows & Light

This blessed progress
Not that of upwards progression,
But of open surrender.
Again, and again
Learning
To let love in.
Forgiving
Letting go of perfection,
The gifts
Are found in love.
The jewels of our inner
Temple
Unlocking ancient
Ways, that bind us together
Parting spaces
Of separation,
Of fear.
Where our humanness
Is steady.
Only here there
Is possibility for movement
In the untangling
Of shadows.
We arrive again to let compassion rise,
Elevating the most broken of hearts.

When we are triggered, challenged, emotionally charged, we have the beautiful opportunity to be present to our experience. From this place we witness what it means to be fully alive. To watch a pattern formed long ago. And we create space. To hold ourselves. In the deepest of compassion. And we can choose to shift the energy. The energy shifts in presence. We are all living, breathing, alchemists. In moments. In practice. We do not control what happens externally. The challenges of our lives might not be our fault, their effect on us, how we internalize them, our reactive patterns; they are our responsibility. *Our inner landscape is our responsibility.* It is our inner garden to tend to, to cultivate and care for so that we may reap the bountiful harvest, the rewards of peaceful, connected, nourished, expansive, grounded and beautiful relationships. The one within us, with the people that mean the most to us and with our global family. With those we know, and those we don't.

Especially with those who challenge our heart. With those who cross our path, the unexpected teachers who illuminate the places we are disconnected from love. We may not like this, we may not choose to have long lunches with these people or share much space, but we can love them, accept them. Because we see our hearts in theirs, our struggle reflected back, we witness their light and choose to love. We can see their pain, because we've met our own. We trust. We can open our eyes to the opportunities that let uncomfortable feelings, fuel change within our heart. We can be angry, alive and charged. AND *we can* tend to these potent energies; quell them consciously. Witness miracles of alchemy. Be graceful, messy, honest, human in thoughts, words *and* actions. Because this is loving. This is progress. *This is our responsibility.* This is the work that matters. And it begins with self compassion. With our own inner work. With us. In the paying attention.

We must first till the soils of sweetness of our own souls. Meet ourselves tenderly, as it is up to each one of us to nourish our own secret gardens. To care for the peaceful relationship, we have on the inside. For then, and only then, may we enable the space, patience and trust required and extend it outwards. *Making conscious choices as we navigate being charged in the world.* To support ourselves, our humanity. This is hard. This is necessary. Our mother earth is asking us to pay attention. We must trust the path. The unfolding. The non-separation. Trust in connection, in unity. And stay with our feelings, in the moments woven throughout our personal history's, our truths that are guiding us and setting us free.

Energy Practice
Sit quietly and reflect.
What practices or rituals do you use (*or want to*) that feel like you're "Tilling the soils of sweetness upon your soul"?
Tune into the feelings that come up in your awareness when you feel into the answers this question asks of you (*follow your heart*). Sit in this energy portal for a few minutes of intentional Self Love charging (*You may even actually choose to take action in this moment and do the practices to help get you into the state of sweetness*). Invite in or continue to use the practices, daily.

May we see them with bright eyes, *our lessons*. May we watch how life exists to help us grow. To expand. So we may learn, soar and sail into new ways of being. Upgrade our energy fields. Move into a new world, a new era. One of loving, witnessing. One of faith. One of balance. *May we watch ourselves rise.* We are emotional beings. We are spiritual beings. We all have big hearts and unique expressions, gifts to share with the world. When we can lean into the divine space we've unlocked, when we awaken to this compassion; we bless ourselves with more opportunities to SHOW UP.

To surrender. *To disarm all the places, we've been disconnected from love.* And connect with our ever abundant light, the light flowing through us, surrounding us. The one ever present and aligned with universal love. We all have this capacity. The ability, to tap in, to shapeshift, to evoke, this gift.

This is our birthright. And it is our duty, our worthy stewardship, in kindness, for all humanity. May we move to the energy in our hearts, feel it in the trees and hear it in the oceans. This *grace* is alive in us all.

There's a brilliance that exists when like hearts breathe voice into forgotten truths and remind us to trust our innate wise elders, who know.

MORNING BLOSSOM

Mother earth is speaking loudly. She asks us now, more than ever, to heal our wise hearts and honour her own, in this *great awakening*.

Birdsong

Why must words
Come, dear one?
Be patient. Be still.
Here you are
Quiet morning
Ripples in the lake,
Curled up and writing

Do not think
You must
Write anything
Profound. For
The essence of
Writing wakes
You

Integrating
The star codes
Meant for you. For
Evolution.
Never seek for more.
Trust in these moments
Unfolding.
Trust in receiving
The beauty
Of this new day.

That this is enough.
That this is the language
Spoken by the angels.
Hear them
Guiding you
Through nature's
Melodies,
Sung in birdsong.

The Mind & Success

Why do I keep chasing you?
Holding onto this belief
And I grasp
So tightly
The spaces Inside
Me have no
Room to breathe.

There's no flow
In the grasping
No ease
With the race,
I'm tired
Of winding myself
Like a top
I can't face

Be still
Spinning waters
Anchor
Your inner lands,
Success is
Not a collection
Of perfectly placed
Moments
Constructed by your hands…

Be free
Darling
in the
Mellows of unfolding
And clear the path
To allow
For just this

Your soul is aching
For the
Clarity uncovered
By believing
In your gifts.

Journaling

What do you feel when you read this poem?

What does true success feel like for your heart? Are there any outdated beliefs or feelings coming up that might be holding you back from experiencing your true success? How do you want to experience success in your life? What are your inner gifts? How do you feel when you share them with the world?

When we decide, to just get quiet. When we decide to trust. When we decide our heart has been right all along. When we decide to surrender, because deep down, we know that it's the only way. When we decide, to commit to our dreams, to answer the call so clear and beautifully radiant in our heart. When we decide, we already know - that we've known all along. This is when there's nothing left to decide. For it's magic here. And the universe, in all it's beauty, it's conspiring, shifting, blooming, beaming, asking us through heart whispers, to bring our dreams to life. That spark of joy that cracks us open. Here, amidst all the madness, life's twists and turns. Here lies the...magic. Right here. And as it was written in the stars, as it's been felt again and again, that feeling in our heart, that knows, that sparkles, that beams brighter than a thousand suns, that knowing, of exactly what needs to shine through us to light the world?

It's here, that's it's already decided, because *we are made of stardust.*

Repeat after me

I have an abundance
Of healing love
Within me

I am capable of shifting my energy

I am love. I am balance.
I am pure wonder.
I am space.
I am healing.

Ritual (mirror work)
Gaze into your favourite mirror, at yourself, and repeat the
affirmation prayers from above *(Start with 1-5 minutes.)*

Radiant being, trust your wise heart.

Elevate, honour and appreciate the gifts that bloom from your garden.

Hello *beautiful soul.* Today is a day to remember. To be gentle and kind with yourself. And as you reflect, as you *befriend the little girl inside you,* the one who is scared. How do you tend to her heart? What does she need? How is she speaking through you today and how can you love her more? Invite her closer. Allow your inner garden to be a safe haven for her to play. Ask her to curl up with you. Under the lilac tree, in the meadow, where she's warm, nurtured and loved. Let her speak and tell you how her heart hurts. And from that space of gentleness and love, you teach each other how to be. Because *love is the only medicine she needs.*

Hello *beautiful soul*. Today is a day to remember. To be gentle and kind with yourself. And as you reflect, as you *befriend the little boy inside you,* the one who is scared. How do you tend to his heart? What does he need? How is he speaking through you today and how can you love him more? Invite him closer. Allow your inner garden to be a safe haven for him to play. Ask him to curl up with you. Under the lilac tree, in the meadow, where he's warm, nurtured and loved. Let him speak and tell you how his heart hurts. And from that space of gentleness and love, you teach each other how to be. Because *love is the only medicine he needs.*

Hello *beautiful soul*. Today is a day to remember. To be gentle and kind with yourself. And as you reflect, as you *befriend the little person inside you,* the one who is scared. How do you tend to their heart? What do they need? How are they speaking through you today and how can you love them more? Invite them closer. Allow your inner garden to be a safe haven for them to play. Ask them to curl up with you. Under the lilac tree, in the meadow, where they're warm, nurtured and loved. Let them speak and tell you how their heart hurts. And from that space of gentleness and love, you teach each other how to be. Because *love is the only medicine they need.*

It's *okay* to have a lot of thoughts.

Darling, if you're tired, be tired. If you're down, be down. When you're bright, shine. Be with what is. Remember it's okay. You are right where you are. Exactly where you need to be. You are alive. Trust this. Know you're taking good care of yourself, trust in the kindness you show your heart. Be, in each moment. Right there. Dare not to dream about being somewhere else - for if you do, your heart, your beautiful heart, it'll be pulled. In two directions. And darling, your heart is asking you, to be pulled only to love. The love found in presence. Seeing clearly, exactly where you are. *As you are.* Moment to moment.

When I slow down, create space to pay attention, connect with my essence and heal my heart. Everything changes. And I'm still healing now, still growing. And it's glorious. And messy. Forever on the path. Rich with possibility. Right here. Choosing love.

We always get what we need and never more than we can handle. It's up to us whether we can see these opportunities for love, through eyes of gratitude.

Divine blessings under the moon revealing sweetness in all it's forms.

Let your wild heart roar amidst the silence.

POETESS, LIONESS

The rituals and practises so dear to the heart, they wait for you always. When you believe that spirit holds you in her patient wings, a canopy of love wraps you up and brings you home.

I remember when it wasn't easy
To love myself.
To let myself bask,
In the light,
Of my broken heart
And what it was teaching me.

I remember when I fell back
Into love.
I let my heart ache,
In the light
Of this journey into love,
And it's awakening.

Journaling
Write about a time you chose to honour Self love above
anything else, however big or small.
Breathe that in, how does it feel?

I allow truth to come out. Even when truth is anger, even when truth is sadness. I trust my feelings; I know they are truth.

When cold winter days tug at your heart, it's okay to dream of palm trees. You are allowed to love the glorious summer sun. But, be present amongst the naked trees and snow, for they are beautiful teachers too.

My heart remained quiet. For a long time. Feeling deeply. It's time to share my roar, to be healed by expressing. Letting truth out. Peace through light and trusting I deserve to speak loudly and take up space. *Letting fierce light flow.*

Affirmations
I am fierce light
I am fierce light
I am made of fierce light
I am fiercely connected to my light.

Poetry speaks the unspoken truths of my heart.

Sing with me darling
Don't quiet your light,
Stay with me darling
In the songs of delight.
Be with the silence,
The space and the trees
In the heart of the light
You'll believe all you seek.

Wild, authentic expression.

Energy Practice
Read the poetic medicine *(above)* again and again, perhaps even speak it out loud. *Wild, authentic expression.* What truth(s) does it evoke in your body, mind and heart? Feel it. Feel them. Breathe in. Breathe out. Really allow yourself to connect and bask in the energy.

Affirm: I trust that my self care practices help me tend to my heart, connect me to my truth and allow the essence of my being to be shared with the world.

There is a softness that anchors the heart to this sweet moment, like a jewel of love that casts rainbows of light upon our wounds and honours our tears.
Breathe into this space.

The wise elder within is aching for trust. Right here. As she holds this heart. Reminding me to stay another moment in the madness. For within the darkness of fear, shame and grief I honour these magical gateways that melt me into the light.

Lean in and trust in what is difficult.
Hold space for yourself
Have the hard conversations,
share your truth because
It matters.
And remember your anxious heart is
Always leading you,
towards where you need to go.

When we hold space
learn to love ourselves fully,
our whole selves | all the parts | the dark | our light
with no judgement,
become our own best friend.
When we lean in | learn to sit
in the discomfort of our shadow | our truth | forgive ourselves
and find kindness | compassion
amidst the wildest of storms
it is here | in this space | where *we are free*
and this is where the magic is.

Finally, an **Energy Practice & Ritual** for all day everyday.
Asking yourself, again and again the following questions:

> *"How can I love myself more in this moment?* And
> *"What do I need right now to love myself more?"*

Thank you for being here.
Thank you for taking up space.
Thank you for letting your light beam
and your heart radiate goodness.
You are here to shine,
you beautiful human.

ENCORE

Choosing happiness, coming and going. Changing by the day. There is pain, there is frustration. *Remember there is steadiness, in the unknown.* The mystery will be filled with music, when your ears are open. Speak about the madness, share this grief out loud. The twisted wave, suspended here, with nowhere else to fall, but the next moment. And the one after that, surrender again. And let your tears dry, by the light of stained glass, its warm hues feeding you and speaking in technicolour. I feel supported here, among the ceilings that capture the air. Breathing sweet, smoky, spiritual offerings into grieving cavities. This season of pain, relieved by becoming the ache that serenades these salted and softened cheeks. A silent smile measuring the willingness to offer love and move these tingling arms around me and into the next moment. In all sound and smells familiar, recognized by this heart. Believing in the rapture of arriving at this place, in these trying times.

This Rainbow is your Home.

There is a line that is crossed through every heartbreak, among the tears that pour. The one you cross, like you've never crossed before. It's waited for you in the shadows and followed you from house to house. Moving, changing, wishing, waiting, for you to choose yourself. Oh dear girl, to love you so much It feels uncomfortable, when often you've known the feelings of what others bring. Step back, slow down, go in and listen to an open heart that sings. This new beginning is changing you, in the wildest of ways. A path your insides have been aching of, always. You don't have to try so hard to make it feel real, its destined in the stars, as you share and feel. So, let's begin again, here, now, together. On this quiet morning in your castle. The weathers steady, whispering to me of your visions and butterfly travels. I'm so proud of the spaces across the waves of magic we've journeyed. I meet you here; the other side of love's churning. So my wise one, may our rhythms be steady as this heart of wisdom safely fastens the yearning. Counteract the anxious and keep us here, unafraid of returning, to the learning.

Alchemy

We are magnetic beings of light,
Rise up to your birthright
These waves
The pulses inside
Showing you the way
Guiding us to the potential
Our ancestors wish for us.
This levelling up
Takes practice,
Takes patience
And resilience
And fortitude.
It takes saying no
to old paradigms
And instead, trusting
The heart's wise elder,
The one divinely connected
To the cycles of the moon
And the breath of humanity.
When we realize that we are
Meant to be born again
From the tragic depths
Bled through discomfort,
Out of fear,
Without carrying the weight
Or burdens of heavily cloaked
Culture comforts.
When we move towards the reform

And say yes
To our own revolution.
The knowing
The trust…

The prosperity
And abundance
That forever waits in the wings,
Readying
Our reclamation
Towards inner authority
Integrity
And the collective good,
This is where we rise.
Leaning in
To the facets of truth
That rip through
Any dark nights of the soul,
So we may emerge from the ash
And believe once more
In this great awakening,
That begins again
In each moment,
On the threshold
Of our deeply ravaged wounds.
Pressuring claims in these unknowns,
Believing spirituality
Is not solely sought in light,
But encouraged in meeting the depths
of darkness...
And choosing,
To let it lead you there.

Favouring all the electric aches
That turn us *to gold.*

Pursue your dreams with fierce curiosity, passion and faith. For only your heart knows, what it aches for. *Take a stand for the wisdom that flows through you* and be relentless on the journey towards love.

Gratitude to all my angels,
who helped birth this book into being.

Heal your heart

Speak your truth

Connect to the wise elder within you

Awaken your wild,

authentic self.

We are *all* alchemists.

REFLECTION & PRAYER

Channeling this book was a gift for my heart. It healed me deeply. It flowed so strongly through me like river water that stops at nothing to forge its path. A collection of present moments. Some, of ease, while most others showed up in heartache, as powerful blocks offering me potent opportunities to stay in the discomfort, to witness the fuel; the spark and flames of this lioness' inner fire. Growth is hard. Transformation is really messy. Creativity is divine. Love is everything.

When we trust in what is difficult, when we learn to sit with ourselves, and stay, it is here, where we awaken the magic in our heartache.

Thank you for being here with me. Thank you for being here with you. *I'll close with a prayer:*

I write for the ones who are unbelievably strong. The ones who hold the whole world in their heart. To the ones who aren't okay. And to the ones who are. And for those who struggle to be at peace with being both. For the beings who have been told it's weak to cry. And for the ones who are called too sensitive when they are met with the flowing river of their tears. I see you. I feel you, you're deep in my heart because I am one of you. And I walk beside you.

It is my wish, for you, for us, the tender, the heartbroken. Those with the weary eyes cast upon weathered gardens. It is my wish, for us, to know the light, to feel it, see it, believe it. Trust it. Become it. For we are made of this light and we are truly supported; blessed beyond measure.
My wish for us, for the sensitive, passionate wild hearts, is to hold space for ourselves, for each other. To be courageous. To share our stories. Our tears, our joys. May we rise together in community to remind ourselves how bright we shine in ALL of our powerful expressions. May our tears be celebrated, our emotions honoured. May the soft feminine, the beautiful masculine, alive within us; in all that we are, be so deeply rooted in our being. May we always know we are enough and not too much; at the same

time. That it's okay to feel. To live fully present to it all, this crazy beautiful journey of the awakened life. To remember this. To witness. To be with what is difficult. And to trust our hearts. To care for them and never forget, that they are teaching us. In every moment. So that we may shimmer, as we bask in the glow of our divine essence; radiating it to the world.

As you move from this moment to the next. May you make space for yourself, to feel fully. To pause. And to breathe. To be with what is. What comes up for you. Here with your life, right now. To stay. To trust in what is difficult, and lean in. To hold yourself in reflection and awaken love. For the experience of our wise truths have many faces. And they are all okay. So remember to celebrate yourself, on this very day, no matter what is present for you. Be here with it. All of it. Move, breathe, pray, sit, rest, write, play. And may the vibrations of love nourish your beautiful soul as they illuminate the path into the light.

Sit up tall, Place your hand on your heart,
Take a deep breath in,
And... *let it go.*

I'm glad you're here. I'm so honoured to share this space with you. Life isn't always easy, but no storm unheard the thunder roar. We come alive when challenges let us sing, ache and soar. We were born to connect to the divine tools, gifts and offerings that support our vital energy. So that when we are asked, to walk through the fire, the medicine, we remember it IS possible to pay attention, become intimate, arrive to the flames in trust. Supported, alive, full up with life's magic mystery, a must. We can let ourselves burn and from it transform, as we watch the smoke clear from the biggest of storms. Then move into the next moment, revealing an inner landscape of peace. When seeing things clearly, we believe all we seek. Deeply supported at rest we remember, to bear witness and *transmute our pain,* in surrender.

For from these shattered achings we arrive in the space, where we get to choose love,
Again, and again.
And it is here, where, all we have is this.
In the continuing…

Because,
We are born again,
Moment to moment;

In the *heart* of the light.

AshleyLord.com

@loveashleylord

loveashleylord@gmail.com

ASHLEY is a Canadian Artist.

A poetess priestess, an intuitive spiritual guide, a wildly sensitive soul; her life is dedicated to divine creative expression. Through her devotional art and in her Sacred Self Care Community she holds powerful space, offering guidance, ceremony and mentorship for all those who seek to transform their darkness into abundant self love. A born adventurer; her Taurean, double Leo heart channels potent, intuitive medicine from the universe. She hails from Toronto but you can find her

...dancing under the moonlight, *writing all the poetry.*

EMOTIONAL FREEDOM TECHNIQUE (EFT) or "Tapping"

Use the tips of your first 2-3 fingers *(pointer, middle & ring)* to tap *(gently)* on different points of the body while repeating affirmations.

Tap just above the eyebrows (both hands):
"It's okay that I feel overwhelmed and/or anxious, I love and accept myself"

Tap just under the eyes, at the top of the cheekbones (both hands):
"It's okay to have these feelings, I love and accept myself"

Tap just under the nose (one hand):
"It's okay that I feel overwhelmed and/or anxious, I love and accept myself"

Tap just under the mouth above the chin (one hand):
"It's okay to have these feelings, I love and accept myself"

Tap onto the collarbones (both hands):
"It's okay that I feel overwhelmed and/or anxious, I love and accept myself"

Tap onto the center of the chest just above the breastbone (one hand):
"It's okay to have these feelings, I love and accept myself"

Tap just below the armpit, at the bra line (one hand):
"It's okay that I feel overwhelmed and/or anxious, I love and accept myself"

Tap onto the top of the head (one hand):
"It's okay to have these feelings, I love and accept myself"

♥

Ashley writes a monthly Love Letter

REGISTER TO READ IT HERE

AshleyLord.com/Love-Letters

♥

Join Ashley's *Sacred Self Care Community*

FIERCE LIGHT SOCIETY

AshleyLord.com/fiercelightsociety

Take yourself on a journey
beyond the mind
where your inner wisdom
works it's magic for the highest good.

Affirm:
I am peaceful and powerful
I am an alchemist
I am capable of unlocking the wisdom of my heart

Remember darling,
you are love.

"I had to really grow out of the victim space. The place that was running the show. I had to *intimately connect* with a fiery young rebel heart alive in me who was caught between blame, anger and shame. I had to learn to re-parent myself in all the ways the little girl within me needed to be loved. Express all that needed to be expressed and learn to listen again to what she had to say. I needed a place where it was okay to have no filter and not worry about inventing a person, I thought I *should* be. I had to thank my beautiful parents, truly fall in love with them again while consciously releasing the energy patterns holding me back from moving forward. A fire needed to burn hard, so I could torch all the rooms I'd let others rent in my home and bathe, in the dust. I had to rage in surrender, to release them as I found out how to rise. I awoke the queen goddess and bowed down to it all, as I watched my voice return again, to its rightful place, on the throne of my heart."

-Ashley Lord, on the three-year healing journey of writing her first book.

ashley lord
heart medicine